OTHER HELEN EXLEY GIFTBOOKS

...And Wisdom Comes Quietly

Timeless Values

A Special Gift of Peace and Calm

The Value of Integrity

Thoughts on Being at Peace

Wisdom for Our Times

Words on Solitude and Silence

In Beauty May I Walk *(Native American Wisdom)*

Published simultaneously in 2005 by Helen Exley Giftbooks
in Great Britain and the USA.

8 10 12 11 9

Selection and arrangement copyright © Helen Exley 2005.
The moral right of the author has been asserted.

ISBN 978-1-86187-147-3

A copy of the CIP data is available from the
Brtish Library on request. All rights reserved.

Words and pictures selected by Helen Exley.
Printed in China.

**Helen Exley Giftbooks, 16 Chalk Hill, Watford,
WD19 4BG, UK.**
For a complete listing of all titles, visit:
www.helenexleygiftbooks.com

TAKING TIME
TO JUST BE

A HELEN EXLEY GIFTBOOK

Each day is a gift
Open it.
Celebrate.
Enjoy it.

STUART & LINDA MACFARLANE

Enjoy life, employ life. It flits away and will not stay.

PROVERB

if we had eyes to see

N ATURE IS PAINTING FOR US,

DAY AFTER DAY,

PICTURES OF INFINITE BEAUTY

IF ONLY WE HAVE EYES TO SEE THEM....

JOHN RUSKIN (1819-1900)

...there's the real danger of overlooking
a very important day... today.
For this is the place and the time for living.
Let us live each day abundantly and beautifully
while it is here.

ESTHER BALDWIN YORK

Always hold fast to the present.
Every situation, indeed every moment,
is of infinite value, for it is the representative
of a whole eternity.

JOHANN WOLFGANG VON GOETHE (1749-1832)

PEACE

Over all the mountaintops
Is peace.
In all treetops
You perceive
Scarcely a breath.
The little birds in the forest are silent.
Wait then; soon
You, too, will have peace.

JOHANN WOLFGANG VON GOETHE (1749-1832)

Even if something is left undone,
everyone must take time to sit still
and watch the leaves turn.

ELIZABETH LAWRENCE

Springs that never dry up

Inside myself
is a place where I live all alone,
and that's where you renew your springs
that never dry up.

PEARL S. BUCK (1892-1973)

To see a World in a Grain of Sand,
And Heaven in a Wild Flower,
Hold Infinity in the palm of your hand
and Eternity in an hour.

WILLIAM BLAKE (1757-1827),
FROM "AUGURIES OF INNOCENCE"

Suppose we went at a slow enough pace... to feel our bodies,
play with children, look openly, without agenda
or timetable into the faces of loved ones....
Suppose we took time each day to sit in silence.
I think if we did those things, the world wouldn't need much saving.

DONELLA H. MEADOWS

EACH DAY THE FIRST DAY: EACH DAY A LIFE.

DAG HAMMARSKJÖLD (1905-1961)

Write it on your heart that every day
is the best day in the year.

RALPH WALDO EMERSON (1803-1882)

Such words as "Death" and "Suffering"
and "Eternity" are best forgotten.
We have to become as simple and as wordless
as the growing corn or the falling rain.
We must just be.

ETTY HILLESUM
(1914-1943)

O GIFT OF GOD! A PERFECT DAY,
WHEREON SHALL NO MAN
WORK BUT PLAY,
WHEREON IT IS ENOUGH FOR ME
NOT TO BE DOING BUT TO BE.

HENRY WADSWORTH LONGFELLOW
(1807-1882)

WORK IS NOT ALWAYS REQUIRED OF A MAN.
THERE IS SUCH A THING AS SACRED IDLENESS,
THE CULTIVATION OF WHICH IS NOW
FEARFULLY NEGLECTED.

GEORGE MACDONALD (1824-1905)

sacred idleness

I expand and live in the warm day like corn and melons.

RALPH WALDO EMERSON (1803-1882)

...to stand and stare

What is this life if, full of care,

We have no time to stand and stare....

No time to turn at beauty's glance,

And watch her feet, how they can dance....

WILLIAM HENRY DAVIES

(1871-1940)

MY HEART IS TUNED TO THE QUIETNESS
THAT THE STILLNESS OF NATURE INSPIRES.

HAZRAT INAYAT KHAN (1882-1927)

Look to this day! For it is life,
the very life of life.
In its brief course lie all the varieties
and realities of your existence:
the bliss of growth, the glory of action,
the splendour of beauty.
For yesterday is already a dream
and tomorrow is only a vision
but today, well-lived,
makes every yesterday a dream of happiness,
and every tomorrow a vision of hope.
Look well, therefore, to this day!
Such is the salutation of the dawn.

FROM THE SANSKRIT

The sacred is not in the sky,
the place of transcendent, abstract principle,
but rather is based on this earth,
in the ordinary dwelling places of our lives,
in our gardens and kitchens and bedrooms.

MARILYN SEWELL, B.1941

PARADISE IS WHERE I AM.

VOLTAIRE (1694-1778)

THE MIRACLE IS NOT TO FLY IN THE AIR,
OR TO WALK ON THE WATER,
BUT TO WALK ON THE EARTH.

CHINESE PROVERB

Take time to be friendly —

It is the road to happiness.

Take time to dream —

It is hitching your wagon to a star.

Take time to love and to be loved —

It is the privilege of the gods.

Take time to look around —

It is too short a day to be selfish.

Take time to laugh —

It is the music of the soul.

OLD ENGLISH PRAYER

Sit
Rest
Work.

Alone with yourself,
Never weary.

On the edge of the forest
Live joyfully,
Without desire.

THE BUDDHA (C.563 B.C.-483 B.C.)

I loaf and invite my soul....

WALT WHITMAN (1819-1892)

How beautiful it is to do nothing,
and then rest afterward.

SPANISH PROVERB

Breathe, drink, taste...

Live in each season as it passes:
Breathe the air, drink the drink, taste the fruit,
and resign yourself to the influences of each.

HENRY DAVID THOREAU (1817-1862)

time to breathe

In the bustle of life. In the pressure of decisions,
peace has become a luxury.
Take it when it comes, and cherish it. It gives you
the time to breathe.
It gives you rest and hope and life.

PAM BROWN, B.1928

You do not need to leave your room....
Remain sitting at your table and listen.
Do not even listen, simply wait.
Do not even wait, be still and solitary.
The world will freely offer itself to you to be unmasked.
It has no choice.
It will roll in ecstasy at your feet.

FRANZ KAFKA (1883-1924)

Sitting...

What life can compare to this?
Sitting quietly by the window,
I watch the leaves fall and the flowers bloom,
As the seasons come and go.

HSUEH-TOU (982-1052)

Sweet Stay-at-Home, sweet Well-content.

WILLIAM HENRY DAVIES (1871-1940)

To watch
the corn grow

To watch the corn grow, and the blossoms set;

to draw hard breath over ploughshare or spade;

to read, to think, to love, to hope, to pray —

these are the things that make people happy.

JOHN RUSKIN (1819-1900)

a place of calm

Even in the heart of a city
there can be a place of calm.
Doors shut and curtains closed,
a light against the dark,
wrapped round in dear, accustomed things
we can withdraw
and find ourselves again.

PAM BROWN, B.1928

There is no calm like a quiet sea
a space of stillness under the width of sky.
A gently shifting flow of shadow.
A silvering.
A breathing silence
that restores the heart.

PAM BROWN, B.1928

When King Pyrrhus prepared for his expedition into Italy, his wise counsellor Cyneas, to make him sensible of the vanity of his ambition: "Well, Sir," said he, "to what end do you make all this mighty preparation?" "To make myself master of Italy," replied the King. "And what after that is done?" said Cyneas. "I will pass over into Gaul and Spain," said the other. "And what then?" "I will then go to subdue Africa; and lastly, when I have brought the whole world to my subjection, I will sit down and rest content at my own ease." "For God sake, Sir," replied Cyneas, "tell me what hinders that you may not, if you please, be now in the condition you speak of? Why do you not now at this instant, settle yourself in the state you seem to aim at, and spare all the labour and hazard you interpose?"

MICHEL DE MONTAIGNE (1533-1592), FROM "ESSAYS"

no empty hours

There are so few empty pages in my engagement pad,
or empty hours in the day, or empty rooms in my life
in which to stand alone and find myself.
Too many activities, and people, and things.
Too many worthy activities, valuable things,
and interesting people. For it is not merely the trivial
which clutters our lives but the important as well.

ANNE MORROW LINDBERGH (1906-2001),
FROM "GIFT FROM THE SEA"

perfect

*These roses under my window
make no reference to former roses or to better ones,
they are for what they are; they exist today.
There is no time to them.
There is simply the rose; it is perfect
in every moment of its existence.
Before a leaf-bud has burst,
its whole life acts,
in the full blown flower there is no more;
in the leafless root there is no less.*

RALPH WALDO EMERSON (1803-1882),
FROM "SELF-RELIANCE"

Today

A shaft of sunlight
at the end of a dark afternoon,
a note in music,
and the way the back of a baby's neck smells....
Those are the important things.

E.B. WHITE (1899-1985)

to be present
in all one does

To be sensual is to respect and rejoice in the force of life itself,

and to be present in all that one does,

from the effort of loving to the breaking of bread.

PHYL GARLAND, FROM "SOUND OF SOUL"

Do we need to make a special effort

to enjoy the beauty of the blue sky?

Do we have to practice to be able to enjoy it

No, we just enjoy it.

Each second, each minute of our lives can be like this.

Wherever we are, any time, we have the capacity

to enjoy the sunshine, the presence of each other,

even the sensation of our breathing.

We don't need to go to China to enjoy the blue sky.

We don't have to travel into the future to enjoy our breathing.

We can be in touch with these things right now.

THICH NHAT HANH, B.1926

the other side

If we had keen vision of all that is ordinary in human life,
it would be like hearing the grass grow or the squirrel's heart beat,
and we should die of that roar which is the other side of silence.

GEORGE ELIOT (MARY ANN EVANS) (1819-1880)

of silence

*People miss their share of happiness,
not because they never found it,
but because they didn't stop to enjoy it.*

WILLIAM FEATHER

stop to enjoy

If you are losing your leisure, look out!
You are losing your soul.

LOGAN PEARSALL SMITH (1865-1946)

IT IS GOOD TO HAVE AN END TO JOURNEY TOWARD;
BUT IT IS THE JOURNEY THAT MATTERS, IN THE END.

URSULA K. LEGUIN, B.1929

Don't evaluate your life in terms of achievements,
trivial or monumental, along the way....
Instead wake up and appreciate everything you encounter
along your path. Enjoy the flowers
that are there for your pleasure. Tune in to the sunrise,
the little children, the laughter, the rain,
and the birds. Drink it all in... there is no way to happiness;
happiness is the way.

DR. WAYNE W. DYER

We all experience
"soul moments" in life –
when we see a magnificent sunrise,
hear the call of a loon,
see the wrinkles in our mother's hands,
or smell the sweetness of a bay.
During these moments,
our body, as well as our brain,
resonates as we experience the glory
of being a human being.

MARION WOODMAN

soul moments

a reverie

It is good to be alone in a garden at dawn or dark

so that all its shy presences may haunt you and possess you

in a reverie of suspended thought.

JAMES DOUGLAS

One should lie empty, open, choiceless a

beach — waiting for a gift from the sea.

ANNE MORROW LINDBERGH (1906-2001)

Time for myself....

Why is it that I find it so hard to take time for myself?

Time to be, rather than time to do.

And often what is urgent elbows its way to the forefront

of my day and the important gets trampled in the rush.

Teach me the art of creating islands of stillness,

in which I can absorb the beauty of everyday things:

clouds, trees, a snatch of music....

Impress upon my mind that there is more to life

than packing every moment with activity,

and help me to fence in some part of my day with quietness.

MARK'S GC

My favorite piece of music
is the one we hear all the time if we are quiet.

JOHN CAGE (1912-1992)

Nobody
sees a flower —
really —
it is so small —
we haven't the time —
and to see
takes time
like to have
a friend
takes time.

GEORGIA O'KEEFFE
(1887-1986)

stretch out
in the shade

*While others miserably pledge themselves
to the insatiable pursuit of ambition and brief power,
I will be stretched out in the shade singing.*

FRAY LUIS DE LEÓN (C.1527-1591)

We tend to be alive in the future, not now.
We say, "Wait until I finish school and get my Ph.D degree,
and then I will be really alive." When we have it,
and it's not easy to get, we say to ourselves,
"I have to wait until I have a job in order to be really alive."
And then after the job, a car. After the car, a house.
We are not capable of being alive in the present moment.
We tend to postpone being alive to the future,
the distant future, we don't know when.
Now is the moment to be alive.
We may never be alive at all in our entire life.

THICH NHAT HANH, B.1926,
FROM "BEING PEACE"

There is, perhaps, no solitary sensation so exquisite

as that of slumbering on the grass or hay,

shaded from the hot sun by a tree,

with the consciousness of a fresh light air

running through the wide atmosphere

and the sky stretching far overhead upon all sides.

LEIGH HUNT (1784-1859)

It is the little shadow which runs across the grass
and loses itself in the sunset.

CROWFOOT (BLACKFOOT)

You will find the deep place of silence
right in your room,
your garden or even your bathtub.

ELISABETH KUBLER-ROSS

silence

Always we hope someone else
has the answer.
Some other place will be better,
some other time it will all turn out well.
This is it.
No one else has the answer.
No other place will be better,
and it has already turned out.
At the centre of your being
you have the answer;
you know who you are
and you know what you want.

LAO TZU, FROM "TAO TE CHING"

The day has been long
boxed in by glass and concrete
deafening with sound,
the mind lost among a thousand minds.
Step into the scent of evening,
the hush of leaves,
the touch of blossom.
The garden gives you back your life.

PAM BROWN, B.1928

At the centre of the most turbulent heart

there is a place of peace, a place beyond time

that cannot be touched by change or loss.

Here in this stillness is rest and healing.

Nothing we suffer, nothing that we fear, can damage its perfection.

Enter this place of peace and learn the purpose of your life —

not wealth or fame, but the recognition of your unity

with all things. Every thing that you have loved is here.

All joy. All good. No living thing has ever been lost to you.

No evil can survive in this clear shining.

PAM BROWN, B.1928

Everything that slows us down
and forces patience,
everything that sets us back
into the slow cycles of nature,
is a help.
Gardening is an instrument of grace.

MAY SARTON (1912-1995)

IN THE ANCIENT WORLD

IT WAS EVER THE GREATEST OF THE EMPERORS

AND THE WISEST OF THE PHILOSOPHERS

THAT SOUGHT PEACE AND REST IN A GARDEN.

SIR GEORGE SITWELL

The best things are nearest:
breath in your nostrils,
light in your eyes,
flowers at your feet,
duties at your hand,
the path of Right just before you.
Do not grasp at the stars,
but do life's plain, common work
as it comes,
certain that daily duties
and daily bread
are the sweetest things in life.

ROBERT LOUIS STEVENSON
(1850-1894)

everyday

The one who masters the grey everyday is a hero.

FYODOR DOSTOYEVSKY (1821-1881)

I have found such joy in things that fill
My quiet days – a curtain's blowing grace,
A growing plant upon a window sill,
A rose fresh-cut and placed within a vase,
A table cleared, a lamp beside a chair.
And books I long have loved beside me there.

AUTHOR UNKNOWN

...in the stones, the trees, and the skies, is a fulfilment
for humanity, a contentment, without which no life
can be satsified or rested in the deepest sense.

BOB BROWN

An inch of time is an inch of gold:
Treasure it.
Appreciate its fleeting nature.

LOY CHING-YUEN

Yesterday has gone.
Tomorrow may never come.
There is only the miracle of this moment.
Savor it. It is a gift.

MARIE STILKIND

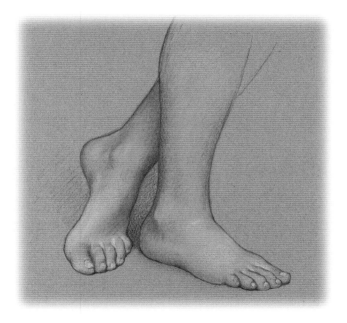

the basic rhythms

Your body is... the expression of your existence....
So many of us are not in our bodies, really at home
and vibrantly present there. Nor are we in touch with
the basic rhythms that constitute our bodily life.
We live outside ourselves — in our heads, our memories,
our longings — absentee landlords of our own estate.

GABRIELLE ROTH

if you listen

Stop for a moment during the day and let the sun
bathe your face. Take a second or two to listen
to the music of the laughter of your children as they play.
Go to a river bank and listen to the sound of the water,
the chirping birds, the blowing of the wind.
It is the world around you that speaks to you,
that will inspire you. If you listen hard enough, you will find
the voice within yourself, and the ability and the power
to make a difference.

ERIN BROCKOVICH, FROM "TAKE IT FROM ME"

There is so much in the world for us all
if we only have the eyes to see it, and the heart to love
it, and the hand to gather it to ourselves....

LUCY MAUD MONTGOMERY (1874-1942)

The most visible creators I know of are those artists whose medium is life itself. The ones who express the inexpressible – without brush, hammer, clay, or guitar. They neither paint nor sculpt – their medium is being. Whatever their presence touches has increased life. They see and don't have to draw. They are the artists of being alive.

J. STONE

life itself

Let us spend one day as deliberately as nature,
and not be thrown off the track by every nutshell
and mosquito's wing that falls on the rails.
Let us rise early and fast, or break fast, gently
and without perturbation;
let company come and let company go,
let the bells ring and the children cry —
determined to make a day of it.
If the engine whistles,
let it whistle till it's hoarse for its pains.
If the bell rings, why should we run?
Time is but the stream I go a-fishing in.

HENRY DAVID THOREAU (1817-1862)

I WISH THAT LIFE SHOULD NOT BE CHEAP,
BUT SACRED. I WISH THE DAYS TO BE AS CENTURIES,
LOADED, FRAGRANT.

RALPH WALDO EMERSON (1803-1882)

Is it so small a thing
To have enjoyed the sun,
To have lived light in the spring,
To have loved, to have thought,
to have done;
To have advanced true friends,
and beat down baffling foes?

MATTHEW ARNOLD

To fill the hour – that is happiness;
to fill the hour, and leave no crevice
for a repentance or an approval.

RALPH WALDO EMERSON (1803-1882)

MORNING

A MORNING-GLORY AT MY WINDOW SATISFIES ME
MORE THAN THE METAPHYSICS OF BOOKS.

WALT WHITMAN (1819-1892)

GLORY

Oh, this is the joy of the rose:
That it blows,
And goes.

WILLA CATHER (1873-1947), FROM "IN ROSE TIME"

ONE BECOMES EMPTY AS THE BEACH

Rollers on the beach, wind in the pines,
the slow flapping of herons across sand dunes,
frown out the hectic rhythms of city and suburb,
time tables and schedules.
One falls under their spell, relaxes,
stretches out prone.
One becomes, in fact, like the element
on which one lies,
flattened by the sea; bare, open,
empty as the beach, erased by today's tides
of all yesterday's scribblings.

ANNE MORROW LINDBERGH (1906-2001),
FROM "GIFT FROM THE SEA"

Do not linger

to gather flowers

to keep them,

but walk on,

for flowers

will keep themselves

blooming all your way.

RABINDRANATH TAGORE
(1861-1941)

walk on...

stop

Don't hurry, don't worry. You're only here for a short visit.
So be sure to stop and smell the flowers.

WALTER HAGEN (1892-1969)

and smell the flowers

If you can spend a perfectly useless afternoon in a perfectly useless manner, you have learned how to live.

LIN YUTANG (1895-1976)

I am gone
into the fields...

I leave this notice on my door
For each accustomed visitor:
"I am gone into the fields
To take what this sweet hour yields;
Reflection, you may come tomorrow."

PERCY BYSSHE SHELLEY (1792-1822)

You ask why I make my home in the mountain forest,
and I smile, and am silent, and even my soul remains quiet:
it lives in the other world which no one owns.
The peach trees blossom. The water flows.

LI PO

ACKNOWLEDGEMENTS
The publishers are grateful for permission to reproduce copyright material. Whilst every effort has been made to trace copyright holders, the publishers would be pleased to hear from any not here acknowledged. ERIN BROCKOVICH: From *Take It From Me*, published by McGraw-Hill, © Erin Brockovich 2002. THICH NHAT HANH: Extracts reprinted from *Being Peace* (1987) by Thich Nhat Hanh, with permission of Parallax Press, Berkeley, California, www.parallax.org. ETTY HILLESUM: From *An Interrupted Life: the Diaries and Letters of Etty Hillesum 1941-43*, Persephone Books, 1999. ANNE MORROW LINDBERGH: Extracts from *Gift From The Sea*, © Anne Morrow Lindbergh 1955, 1975, renewed 1983 by Anne Morrow Lindbergh. Published by Pantheon Books and Random House UK Ltd.

LIST OF ILLUSTRATIONS
Helen Exley Giftbooks would like to thank the following organizations and individuals for permission to reproduce their pictures: AKG-Images (AKG); The Bridgeman Art Library (BAL), Edimedia (EDM); The Fine Art Photographic Library (FAP); Getty Images; Scala; Superstock. Whilst every reasonable effort has been made to trace copyright holders, the publishers would be pleased to hear from the any not here acknowledged.

Page 66: *Une Vallee, Effet du Matin*, ANTOINE CHINTREUIL
Page 138: ARTIST UNKNOWN
The publishers have been unable to trace the copyright holders for these pictures and would be grateful if the representatives for these artists could contact them.

Front Cover, Title Page and Endpapers: *November Moon, Wigeon with the Tide*, JULIAN NOVOROL, private collection, BAL

Page 6: *Winter Sunset through the Trees*, ROBERT HALLMANN, BAL

Page 8: *The River*, YVONNE DELVO, Osbornes Collection, BAL

Page 10: *Thawing Ice on the Lysaker River*, FRITZ THAULOW, BAL

Page 12: Spring, JAMES HERBERT SNELL, FAP

Page 14: *Port-Marly, White Frost*, ALFRED SISLEY, Palais des Beaux-Arts, Lille

Page 16: *Man leaning on a Parapet*, GEORGE PIERRE SEURAT, BAL

Page 18: *Etude des Mains*, EDGAR DEGAS, Superstock

Page 20: *Down to the Sea*, TIMOTHY EASTON, BAL

Page 22: *Golden Autumn*, ISAACK ILYICH LEVITAN, BAL

Page 24: *Marooned*, HOWARD PYLE, BAL

Page 26: *Stiller Wintertag*, MAX CLARENBACH, Galerie Paffrath

Page 28: *Drifting Clouds*, CASPAR DAVID FRIEDRICH, BAL